# BLOODLINE

ALSO BY ADRIAN BLEVINS

*The Man Who Went Out for Cigarettes (chapbook)*
*The Brass Girl Brouhaha*
*Live from the Homesick Jamboree*

# BLOODLINE

## A Chapbook

Adrian Blevins

Hollyridge Press
Venice, California

Hollyridge Press
Venice, California
www.hollyridgepress.com

Cover Design and Book Design by Rio Smyth
Cover Art by Adrienne Beacham
Author photo by Connie Stevens
Manufactured in the United States of America by Lightning Source

ISBN-13: 978-0-9843100-6-7
ISBN-10: 0-9843100-6-1

I am grateful to the editors who first published many
of the poems in this collection, most in earlier versions:

*Appalachian Studies*: "Hullabaloo"

*Exit 7: A Journal of Literature and Art*: "Kid Icarus," "Problem Child," and "Ars Poetica"

*Georgia Review*: "Tally"

*Gulf Coast*: "Walking It Off"

*Massachusetts Review*: "Tongue-Tied at Sea" (as "Motherhood")

*White Whale Review*: "The Plunge," "And Then the Babies Began to Wiggle and Drop," and "Testimony"

*Zone 3*: "Memo," "This Little Catalogue of Losses," and "Bloodline"

"Tally" also appeared on Poetry Daily (www.poems.com) and won a Pushcart Prize. It will appear in *Pushcart Prize XXXVII Best of the Small Presses*.

20 19 18 17 16 15 14 13 12     10 9 8 7 6 5 4 3 2 1

# Contents

# BLOODLINE

# THE PLUNGE

You can stand on the brink of the gorge and jump
   if you like your bathing suit. If the water's not too far,
      too hot, too fat with the pee foam of cattle or fish

and the soggy bodies of boys, girls, men, women
   and the Spartan elderly with their floating picnic debris
      of supple infant charges and *their* toy guns

and other bright orange pacifiers floating in the creek
   you went to in '78 sometimes for fun you guess
      or really because you were after negligence

as in to find a joint and smoke it, a beer and drink it,
   a boy to do him with a Chevy to speed in
      or a Ford to get way down and hide in

because in point of fact your bathing suit was kind
   of nasty, came from Texas or some other trash heap
      or discount barrel or psychotic middle drawer

of birthed-out cat blood and fur ruminant
   and just try to say otherwise, you nebulous little idiot,
      you long-ago fuss I think of poof I think and whoosh.

# TESTIMONY

Her desire for the babies diminished
   after she had them, though naturally
      they were still there,

teeming like microbes in every muddy place
   she'd pick them up to ponder
      their outlandish qualities

such as they were full of angle and craving
   like those quilted squares of rice
      she used to toss in the gym

at school. Such as: water enraged them.
   And any kind of rubbing
      or sheering. Not to mention

the middle of the night with the moon up there
   being too vigorous a thing
      to sleep through. Ditto

peas from a can and corn from a can
   and anything at all
      even lightly slack,

as another snag as regards the babies
   was them always wanting down
      when they were up and up

when they were down. As in: they were
   foolish! And messy! And made all spoiled and knotty
      the simplest activities

such as drinking tea or walking unmindfully
   not to even mention the bother
     of their constant requirements

such as rubber pants and fruit cups
   not to even mention their beds and dolls
     and things to jump on and listen to

as well as the shots against diphtheria and tetanus
   and the gathering of other meds
     for the insomnia and diarrhea

making their poor mother
   inasmuch as destitute
     unless you consider her

always doing this song of them
   all doleful and doting
     and fucked-up and fraught.

# ARS POETICA

She was not blissful in that garden. Not
blissful harvesting it. Not blissful not.
She was not blissful not inseminated,
and couldn't stand getting vast. She
didn't like the godforsaken vaccinations:
Christ, how those children wept! She
didn't like when school was canceled,
and she liked it even less when it was
not. The very best was just before she went
to sleep, where it doesn't matter who you
are. That's when she'd lie like an old dog
in a ditch, and, yeah, she's happy saying this.

# AND THEN THE BABIES BEGAN
# TO WIGGLE AND DROP

and wander like swine on the floor of the bank
   and in every you-name-it field and aisle I guess because

whatever I had or was the thankless little cannibals
   didn't want any more as in not milk and not peas or sleep or stories

and not their dad either or any person anywhere because
   if you'll pardon the expression, the babies thought that this was

the shit—whatever this was—this moving on the ground
   so loose and wobbly, this feeling so unfastened and variable,

this lax and spur-of-the-moment and even slightly squalid sense
   of the unchained knees corresponding to the ground

                with the face and things all airy and out

unless that's wrong and I'm worse than mistaken
   and we were all quite fretful and shell-shocked back then

like we were all blasted up from some thunderous vault
   and I'm not saying we were and I'm not saying we

weren't, but us being a family back then may have been like us
   being on a little boat rocking to and fro

when it was always winter or it was worse than hot
  and our skin would get stuck together ripping holes

when we'd part and I'm not saying this was my incarceration
  because I was too devoted and as for my heart pounding

    like a pounding wanting out, so what, so what, so what?

# HULLABALOO

Things would get a little more fascinating
        when the babies got sick:

when fret would flip her open

like a latch. If the babies were hot
        she would warily

undress them. If the babies were dry

she would just as cagily but with
        her own body

feed them. And if the babies threw up

she would sponge them all over
        with a little lawless washing rag.

This is how she would get out of herself,

where in case you were wondering
        she's incredibly trapped.

# TALLY

The babies smelled like mixed-up milk and cotton dragged
through a little wax, but not like sugar or any amount

of caramel. Smelled like salty pee and skin swabbed slick
and the years forthcoming lit up by lemons. Smelled

like not-death—like the earliest of the early yield—like
kale and collards, maybe. Like lettuce? Smelled like

soil, though not so wholly-hearted—smelled more like
fallen apples, I would say, or melons rotting in baskets

made of a tincture of wheat and river water and were thus
like sleep in an antique pantry. I mean, were like sleep

that much at last. Were sleep unchained from trees
and time and fire and time and hunger and time plus time

plus longing—were sleep cut loose from up and down
and this and that and therefore were—the asinine things—

life at its most extreme and comatose and dragging and slap-
dash—yes—but thunderstruck, all the same. And yes. And best.

# MEMO

Even the large babes were small.

They were like two empty toilet paper tubes you glue together into a bazooka to blow at the cosmos through.

They were like hummingbirds on a spit.

Hummingbirds, goldfinches, wrens—something that's got its feathers all wet in the rain out there and the wind.

This was back when I was still so young and even more combustible—when all I wanted was to sit on the ledge to the left there and drink a little and smoke.

That is, I was a big fretter—I had a worried brain—I couldn't stop counting what was nineteen inches long—nineteen or twenty—like the foot plus not even the whole calf of my little sister.

Like certain black roasting pans in my mother's pantry.

Like her dark green throw pillows not exactly everywhere.

Like the trees in the back of the house that worked so hard to be tall and kill pansies.

Like the balusters of banisters spinning on the table in the cabinetmaker's shop.

Maybe that's where they'd make the elfin casket, if it came to that.

I wanted something honest and plain—pine, maybe—something with a texture of goose down as it degraded to sawdust so the baby's littleness could be married inside that darkness to some kind of softness like frayed wheat.

This was when I was twenty-two.

I had, as the saying goes, my whole life to look forward to.

The new little thing was giggling over there on a blanket—eyeing the world as it flitted and sang.

The new little thing was all hot sequin and dazzle and cute pee flaunt.

Nobody was dying.

Nobody was even the slightest bit sick.

Still I sat there wedged inside myself waiting for whatever gods to come on and ruin it.

That is, as regards the serrated heaviness I seem to have to carry along inside me with its old edge hanging like a leaf from the top of the collarbone to a certain nervy line just above the pubes.

I am talking about what feeling that feels like.

What having the little ones did to me and how much each trifling half inch as they would grow would ache.

It is twenty-seven bobby pins in a long, bloody row.

It is a spatula.

It is a rotting harrow.

It is the plough and the rake.

It is the spade.

# TONGUE-TIED AT SEA

I'd be a lot better off saying what things are sort of like if my bad attitude—that buzz,
that hum—didn't keep coming back like some old rain, especially on a day like today
with all the moisture in and around and above and below so many clouds
I may as well be in a white painting in a long dress on a small boat in the middle
of the moist, moist sea. But there is remorse here—I'll give you that—and time
somehow so untidy I can't remember what I did or didn't do, though there are ropes here
since there are fishermen and since with fishermen come nets. Not to even mention
the three children like the wings of moths poking in at me while I drift a little drunk
above the aquamarine surface as yes I had them and yes I meant to save them and no I
couldn't, maybe because I was at the core of this other thing—this buzz, this hum—
running hard after it and trying therein to vanquish it by trying to get at it. And yes people
were hungry and there were too many cats and trash and yes this is the shame and the
        dumb trouble
I don't want to talk about. And while it's not what you'd call all bombs and annihilation,
it *is* accident after accident with just that same kind of randomness and light yellow
        wretchedness
and lichen-covered stones I think with dusk falling after that like always like ash.

# KID ICARUS

I come from a family of rowdies who don't know their asses
some days from a hole in the ground and in this assessment

I include myself and my offspring so yes my son was drinking beer
late one night on his roof like the kids in that college town like to do

so they can mimic the stars is what I think and talk and dance
for all I know and sing. But the ladder leading up the wall

off the back deck of his apartment looked like pipes you put
water through, only blacker and thinner. And it's warm in Virginia

a lot of the time now and in that heat like rivulets of invisible gas
and in that stupid heat like the air-flow of the chalky untellable

down the boy came like thousands of others painting their houses
and putting up Christmas lights and skiing or just walking along

The Blue Ridge Parkway and just flinging themselves over
down past the evergreens because life can be galling, a sickness,

something you might as well toss willy-nilly over a mountain
and something that can also just randomly plummet

if you inherited your mother's propensity for bare feet and the ladder
is skeletal and gaunt and the moon is pointing toward Japan

and maybe there are crickets chirping, maybe your neighbors
are cranking up the James Brown, maybe fucking and moaning, maybe

slapping, yelling, cursing the day they were ever born and *yadda yadda*
like they say on TV and *yadda yadda life has its limits* like the great poet says

and still it's all but untellable when your child falls twenty-five feet
off the top of a building and lands on the sidewalk face-down

and lives amazingly yes and becomes a so-called "walking miracle" yes I know
but that's still not the cause and effect of the whole cataclysmic tale

when there is remaining this mother sleepless when the moon
is pointing toward Japan and this mother sleepless in bed with the falling

like a racket all the time all around, the boy's rag-doll head face down,
his rag-doll legs spread out, his arms swaying like long rag-doll rags

until he's just his hat and his hat is just the green wind and he's an antique
pencil drawing, is what it comes down to: in my head all the time now

my boy is a smear of wax, a breath, a scatter of escapee powder. Oxidization.
Panic. The gasping fibers of the filaments of bird wing and dust.

# PROBLEM CHILD

I have never written political poetry. I've just rallied against it.
I have not until this very second worn my reading glasses. And no,
I have not been hospitalized for two months or until it happened
hospitalized a child for two months or written the word *hospitalized*
three times in one sentence. It changes everything—*hospitalized,*
*hospital, hospice*—reiterating as it does what I, staring out the window
in the house in Maine at the end of the street on the north side of town,
now realize I was sensing back home in the heat under the tree at thirteen
as regards the lilac dying and the blackberry dying and everything alive
just one day dying and *dying,* to be precise. Because while the point of the oak
was to conceal me from the outlandish individuals lining up for cocktails
and pulling at their pantyhose and preparing their chins to open their mouths
for olives and pâté, there was no tree big enough to cast a shadow long enough
for me to shun the waning frogs and luckless cats and dogs and old people
and children especially wheezing inside their poorly lungs, though of course
I had to suppress all this as everyone in Virginia pretended paradise
and I was told to quit my stupid huff and get inside the house
and please pour, if I would be so kind, the goddamned lemonade.

# THIS POEM WOULD BE ABOUT MY PTSD

if the Yankee populace colonizing the ball field of my small town
    had not gone on and stuffed themselves with more or less Witch Hazel
        and with somehow the many edges of a range of fabrics

as well as I think brushwood and a little pile of wine. I mean,
    just look at the lawn chairs housing the sporty Americans
        as they cheer on the not-chess players and the not-bassoonists

while bemoaning the one-sidedness of the referees! So though
    I sort of want to verbalize the awful feeling like a throbbing
        or maybe like a thrumming that batters yes

and thrashes more than a smidgen and bruises in massive traces,
    these fine Americans could not care less
        about the vast insensitivities of themselves and everyone on earth

going all the way back to way before Tonya Harding
    and thus will never heed the repugnant root cellar of the big quandary here
        hotly wrong like a vehemence is what I think, and just as trembling.

# BLOODLINE

O, high as crazy hell and blasé like rocks was how he seemed to want to play it
there in the hospital with his hands knit loose behind his head and the one leg
lying straight across the other like he was testing a lounge chair or working on his tan
rather than becoming a flashing series of tubes and wires in a bed and comatose
in point of fact in the ICU where the universe gets so mean it blathers like a baby.
Oh, just hanging out and peeing off this country porch, Mom. Just pouring
a little juice into this carroty Hardee's glass on the sun-bleached Formica
the body said in its minute gestures as the nurses stripped it and eyed each other
and counted the numbers and wrote in black ink on white charts and pinched him
to try to wake him and said his name over and over to try to wake him
and called in the priests just in case and diagnosed the smell which was pneumonia
and got the technicians to cart in the machines to get some pictures and injected him
with Penicillin and Percocet and Demerol and Morphine and all the holy waters
and the holy sugars and the proteins and the very important chemical fats. But there
was something about the bloodline that I saw too in my son and came here to say
before I die—something about my own mother's faraway gaze that I could see
in the boy's shut eyes and broken jaw and my own shutdown and blacked-out
old self there too in his wounded and unflappable smashed-up oblivion.

# THIS LITTLE CATALOGUE OF LOSSES

is an old burlap sack that I soaked in pee and stuffed under the bed
so it could possess the fusty venom I consider crucial for the remembering of

(1) my lost youth which was my innocence and which smelled roughly of cedar and
      cinnamon
and (2) my optimism which was as flaxen and delicate as the wooly air above something
      opaque

and (3) my wildness which really was as wayward as the white flora of the mountain laurel
assailing the bootleg vicinity. And into this old sack that is in actual fact

a candid if partial register of my hitherto losses let's put (4) time too
or at least (5) some of the words for it like the *minutes* and the *hours* and the *days* and
      even the *seconds*

I had then that I don't have now, though sooner or later you learn that another word for *lost*
is *gone* and that another word for *gone* is *tender* as in *knocked out* as in *grief-struck*

as in what it all adds up to, which is just a sideways forest called Hard Times
from which comes some tinny music from a high lonesome fiddle or from in my glum case

the guitar my father played before he went missing, another word for which is *died*. So
      please
for my poor father's sake accept the insertion into this catalogue the real scarcity
      evermore

of the apparatus that wasn't the steel thing people play on their laps called a Dobro
but was rather (6) something high-up and slow but spirited in Daddy's voice that people
      call a twang

and which is gone almost completely now from (7) my own talking like my (8) Buster
    Browns
are gone from my feet and (9) my clarinet is gone totally from my heart like (10) my tape
    recorder

and (11) my Kingston Trio that was my father's trio really, so I shall say in conclusion
my (12) Hank as in my Williams as in (13) my grainy tape deck as in (14) my blue Toyota

as in (15) all those long and meandering back roads that got me here
with just a little something luckily leftover out of which frowzled tonight to mourn.

# WALKING IT OFF

Whenever I try to maybe just breathe
   some appalling shit happens
      and I have to get on the couch

and pretend to recover. Even when the trouble slows
   I'm a light bulb with a skull fracture,
      a brick in a way in a dumb-dirty river

being lobbed by semi-kids in splashy shorts
   and bobby pins. And yes being tossed
      wounds the poor viscera

and no we should not be so self-important
   as to think in the plural first person
      as yes we know

we are not the protagonist of the story
   or even a semicolon
      in the middle of a sentence about it

as what really matters is America and *her* heartaches,
   *her* girls on rollerskates. Yes the moon landing
      and yes the GDP.

O Michael Jackson O Walter Cronkite O Natasha
   Richardson: what was it like
      that last second

in the US among us? Was there
   a rope to grab or was it a staircase of mist
      and did you climb to outer space

or was it more like being knocked out
  and carried into the woods
    and thrown into a ditch

or should I imagine each of you wrapped
  in receiving blankets after being
    milked and powdered

or should I think up ants and other insects—
  weevils—crawling your bodies
    and what do you miss

the most? Your skin, your mouths, your
  unique way of thinking with the radio low
    and you smoking at the ravine all hot and giddy

or is it something more unspeakable
  such as your glee of the speed at which
    you rose and flew I guess

and left us so ramshackle and lowdown and droning and loose?

www.ingramcontent.com/pod-product-compliance
Lightning Source LLC
LaVergne TN
LVHW041210080426
835508LV00008B/888